This edition copyright © 2002 Lion Publishing
Text copyright © 2002 Sarah Medina

Published by
Lion Publishing plc
Mayfield House, 256 Banbury Road,
Oxford OX2 7DH, England
www.lion-publishing.co.uk
ISBN 0 7459 4655 0

First edition 2002
10 9 8 7 6 5 4 3 2 1 0

All rights reserved

Acknowledgments

15, 44: Isaiah 45:5; Psalm 16:11, from the Good News Bible published by
The Bible Societies/HarperCollins Publishers Ltd, UK © American Bible
Society 1966, 1971, 1976, 1992, used with permission. 18a: Isaiah 30:15,
from The New Revised Standard Version of the Bible, Anglicized Edition,
copyright © 1989, 1995 by the Division of Christian Education of the
National Council of the Churches of Christ in the United States of
America, and used by permission. All rights reserved. 18b, 45: Psalm 46:10;
Philippians 4:12, from the *Holy Bible, New International Version*, copyright ©
1973, 1978, 1984 by International Bible Society. Used by permission.

Every effort has been made to trace and acknowledge copyright holders of
all the quotations in this book. We apologize for any errors or omissions
that may remain, and would ask those concerned to contact the publishers,
who will ensure that full acknowledgment is made in the future.

A catalogue record for this book is available
from the British Library

Typeset in 12/14 Venetian 301
Printed and bound in China

calm

a way through stress

Sarah Medina

Contents

● ● ● ● ● ● ● ● ● ● ● ● ● ● ● ● ● ● ●

Introduction

• • • • • • • • • • • •

Do you often feel frustrated, exhausted, tense and unhappy with life? Do you find it difficult to relax and switch off? Stress is an unfortunate, but all too common, side effect of life today. In a rush-rush world, speed seems to be of the essence, pushing many beyond their ability to cope.

The symptoms of stress vary from individual to individual. Common physical reactions include aches and pains, a change in appetite, nausea, constant tiredness, heart palpitations, and unremitting susceptibility to illnesses such as colds and infections. People under stress may feel anxious, irritable, unable to concentrate, lethargic, panicky, worried over little things or overwhelmed by life itself. Relationships may suffer, and well-being is severely affected.

The triggers for stress can also vary. Everyone has a different stress threshold. What for some people may be stimulating and even exciting, others may find just too much to deal with. Major life events, both positive and negative, are recognized as being potential triggers for overload: bereavement, divorce, serious illness, marriage, having children or retirement. But little things – small, everyday concerns – may also add up and up until stress takes over.

In the face of all life's pressures, wonderfully, there are things that we can do to reduce our stress levels. Life, with all its ups and downs, is a gift for each of us. Even when we are feeling swamped, we can lift up our heads and see a way out. This is one of the wonders of being human! We are not at the mercy of life; we can learn from our experiences, adopt new strategies and adapt our lifestyles.

This little book will help to show you how. It will encourage you to find strength, space, energy, support, control and, ultimately, calm.

I wish you well on your journey.

Finding strength

The first thing to understand when dealing with stress is that, however you may feel, you have the strength to find solutions and make them work for you. At first you may need to take small steps, it's true. But small steps take you to your destination as well as large ones!

You have much more resilience than you think. To encourage this resilience to flourish, you need to be gentle and patient with yourself. Think positive thoughts; banish negativity! There is no room for self-blame or guilt. There is no space for 'oughts' and 'shoulds', or for comparisons with others. You are learning to love and respect yourself as a unique and valuable person, whatever your circumstances.

By taking simple steps, you can unclutter mind and soul and discover the inner strength that will carry you through. Build yourself up: make sure that you do something you enjoy every day; reward yourself for each achievement; write notes, lists and reminders so that you don't have to strain to remember all you have to do. And don't forget that you can ask for strength, too, from a God who is with you from moment to moment.

There are no hopeless situations;
there are only people who have grown
hopeless about them.

Clare Boothe Luce

Perseverance is not a long race; it is
many short races one after another.

Walter Elliott

When you have gone so far that
you can't manage one more step,
then you've gone half the distance
that you're capable of.

Greenlandic proverb

Start with what you can do;
don't stop because of what you
can't do.

Author unknown

Trust the clarity with which
you see what you have to do.

Henri Nouwen

In the depth of winter, I finally
learned that within me there lay
an invincible summer.

Albert Camus

Whether you think you can or you can't,
you're right!

Henry Ford

You can transcend all negativity when you
realize that the only power it has over you
is your belief in it. As you experience this
truth about yourself you are set free.

Eileen Caddy

If I really want to improve my situation, I can work on the one thing over which I have control – myself.

Stephen Covey

God promises, 'I will give you the strength you need.'

The Bible

Be positive about yourself.

Sally-Ann Lipson

It doesn't matter when you start, as long as you start now.

W. Edwards Deming

Finding space

'*Space?*' you may ask. Space is often the last thing we have when we are under stress.

And yet one of the best things you can do is to take time to stop and think. Finding space to reflect on your situation can help you to gain perspective and insight into what you need to do, and how. Don't be afraid of what might come up when you stop; remember, you have the strength to deal with anything.

And take time out to relax. Deep breathing is a quick and simple technique that can be very powerful. Take a slow, deep breath through your nose, filling your lungs to capacity without straining, and then release the breath slowly through your mouth. Repeat this process a few times. Do this regularly throughout the day, and you will be amazed at how calming it can be!

Because stress can be so tiring, allow yourself to have regular rest periods. Take time to put your feet up, if only for a few minutes. Do all you can to sleep well at night – a good night's sleep will refresh you and strengthen you.

Remember, a little bit of space goes a very long way.

For fast-acting relief,
try slowing down.

Lily Tomlin

In quietness and in trust
shall be your strength.

The Bible

Be still, and know that
I am God.

The Bible

Sleep is the friend of man.

Charles Péguy

Sleep is necessary to renew
the body's strength, and to
rest and refresh the mind.

George Appleton

Sleep, O gentle sleep,
Nature's soft nurse.

William Shakespeare

Moments alone are a life-giving force.

Anne Wilson Schaef

It is part of being truly human that we should create for ourselves oases of stillness in which we can be refreshed.

Tom Wright

To the quiet mind all things are possible.

Meister Eckhart

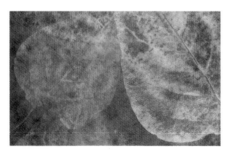

Solitude permits the mind to feel.

William Wordsworth

The quieter you become, the more
you can hear.

Baba Ram Dass

• •

Still, very still.
Now I am ready for hearing God.
Now I am ready for listening.
Now I am ready to talk to him.
Still, very still.

Author unknown

Finding energy

● ● ● ● ● ● ● ● ● ● ● ●

When you are stressed, it is more important than ever to look after yourself. Regular rest and good sleep are important, and we have touched on these already. It is also valuable to think carefully about food, exercise and fun.

How you eat is as important as *what* you eat. When under stress, it is all too easy to rush or skip meals. Regular mealtimes and nutritious snacks are vital. Eat lots of fruit, vegetables, protein and carbohydrates. Snack on healthy options such as nuts and seeds. Drink plenty of water, and avoid caffeine and alcohol. Herbal and fruit teas are tasty alternatives.

Exercise is known to provide relief from stress. There is no need to overdo it. Just choose an activity that you enjoy – walking, swimming or yoga, for example – and begin to incorporate regular slots of 20 minutes or so into your weekly routine.

Having fun is also crucial, even though you may feel that all your laughter switches have been turned off! Build some fun time into your life. You could watch a comedy film, listen to a humorous programme on the radio or read a light-hearted book. Get together with your most cheerful friends, and watch your stress melt away.

Your body tackles stress much better when it's got the energy to do so.

Paul McGee

If you feel stressed, now is the time to build up your stamina by keeping fit.

Gillian Butler and Tony Hope

Improving general health and fitness can protect against and lessen the effects of stress.

Greg Wilkinson

● ● ● ● ● ● ● ● ● ●

Exercise confers emotional benefits through its ability to improve our feelings of mastery, competence and control.

Raj Persaud

The effects of exercise are cumulative, and lots of small sessions are as useful as an hour in the gym.

Jit Gill

Exercise releases the brain's natural opiates, producing calmness and a happier state.

Raj Persaud

Rest means not working. It does *not* mean doing your work sitting on the sofa whilst listening to music. Nor does it necessarily mean doing nothing.

Gillian Butler and Tony Hope

Make G.U.I.L.T. work positively for you in future by remembering it stands for:

Give yourself
Uninterrupted
Indulgent
Leisure and pleasure
Time at least twice a week!

Paul McGee

Muscles throughout the body
tense and relax during laughter,
in exactly the same way as with
stress reduction techniques
such as yoga.

Paul McGee

Laughter is like the human
body wagging its tail.

Anne Wilson Schaef

We are to give our heart to God
that he may make it happy, with
a happiness which stretches its
capacity to the full.

Gordon S. Wakefield

Finding support

When you are under a lot of stress, you may not even recognize what is happening to you. The support and perspective of others can be of enormous help in leading you to a greater understanding of yourself, your situation and the way forward.

You may feel so overwhelmed that you need to seek the advice of a doctor or counsellor. Those who are professionally trained have a great deal of experience in helping people under stress.

Remember, too, that those close to you can be an invaluable help, both emotionally and practically. Call on family and friends; do not cut yourself off from them. You may need a listening ear and a fresh viewpoint. You may need simply to enjoy the company of those who care for you, a pleasurable distraction from all your worries. You may need to ask for practical support, requesting help with some of your tasks. You are not alone; do not be afraid to turn to others.

God is there for you too. In the haste of life, you may forget this. But God does not forget you. God is there for you to unburden your soul, to clarify your thinking, and to bring you peace and calm.

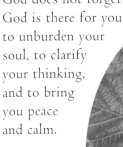

A blessed thing it is for any man
or woman to have a friend, one
human soul we can trust utterly.

Charles Kingsley

Trouble shared is trouble halved.

Dorothy L. Sayers

Friendship is a sheltering tree.

Samuel Taylor Coleridge

God will send to you the people with
whom you can share your anguish.

Henri Nouwen

What do we live for, if it is not to
make life less difficult for each other?

George Eliot

A mile walked with a friend contains
only a hundred steps.

Russian proverb

Many things are lost for
want of asking.

English proverb

People aren't mind-readers.
They can only give you
what you want if you tell
them clearly what that is.

Sally-Ann Lipson

Friends are needed both
for joy and sorrow.

Yiddish proverb

If you're struggling on your own to face challenges, then you need to know you're not alone! 'The God of all comfort is with you.'

Richard Daly

Do not be discouraged. Be sure that God will truly fulfil all your needs. Keep remembering that.

Henri Nouwen

God is always near you and with you.

Brother Lawrence

Finding control

Stress can lead to avoidance and procrastination, so that problems are left unresolved and thus become bigger and even more stressful. It can be a bitter cycle.

You *can* take control, however. Facing up to problems and then keeping them in perspective are key strategies to resolving stress. Even if you are unable to change circumstances, you can change the way you think about them.

Think about your values, goals and priorities. What is important to you? How do you want to live your life? Being clear about these issues will mean that you are in a much better position to decide what and what not to do with your life.

Think about your worries in the long term. Will these things matter in ten years, or even in a year's time? Think about the pressures you face. Can you resolve them? Be realistic. Let go of the things you are not responsible for, or whose solutions are in the hands of others.

Take responsibility – and take action! Take a problem-solving approach to all your worries. Define the problem. Then brainstorm as many possible solutions as you can. Decide on what to do – and do it.

You can do it!

Every moment you have a choice, regardless of what has happened before. Choose right now to move forward, positively and confidently, into your incredible future.

Author unknown

Action springs not from thought, but from a readiness for responsibility.

Dietrich Bonhoeffer

If life gives you lemons, make lemonade.

Dale Carnegie

- I began to think, and to think is one real advance from hell to heaven.

  Daniel Defoe

- I discovered I always have choices and sometimes it's only a choice of attitude.

  Judith M. Knowlton

- In tense situations, tell yourself, 'I can't handle everything, but I am in charge of my attitude, and I choose to relax.'

  Richard Daly

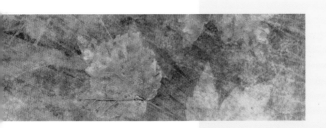

Worry is like a rocking chair.
It will give you something to do,
but it won't get you anywhere.

Author unknown

Worrying is carrying a burden
God never intended us to bear.

Author unknown

Holding onto worries keeps you
feeling vulnerable. Life will feel
calmer when you let them flow by.

Gillian Butler and Tony Hope

Getting stuck is a wonderful place to be because it is a prerequisite to being unstuck.

Mike Yaconelli

We can change, slowly and steadily, if we set our will to it

Robert H. Benson

Character – in things great and small – is indicated when a man pushes with sustained follow-through what he feels himself capable of doing.

Johann Wolfgang von Goethe

To gain that which is worth having, it may be necessary to lose everything else.

Bernadette Devlin

I have accepted all, and I am free. The inner chains are broken as well as those outside.

Charles F. Ramuz

The only way to grow is to
let go.

Anne Wilson Schaef

It may encourage you to think,
'What was the best thing that
happened to me today?' at the
end of each day.

Richard Daly

It is a help to have something
to do, and not to creep about
in a dim fatiguing dream of
anxiety.

A.C. Benson

It never hurts your eyesight to
look at the bright side of life!

Richard Daly

Finding calm

• • • • • • • • • • • • • •

In the maelstrom of stress, calm can
seem a very long way away. But it is
achievable. You have already started
on the path to calm by
reading this book. You now
need to put the suggested
strategies into place, and
you will get there!

Calm is a beautiful place
to be, a place to rest, relax
and enjoy all the gifts that
we have received. It is a
place where we can lie back,
put our feet up and say,
'OK, it doesn't matter what
comes my way, today or in
the future; I can handle it
all with equanimity, poise and
confidence.'

And, believe me, you can! You have
everything you need close by you:

inner resourcefulness, love and
friendship – and God, who truly
cares. Call on these, at any time,
and trust that life is good.

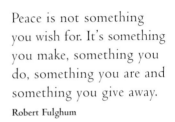

Peace is not something
you wish for. It's something
you make, something you
do, something you are and
something you give away.

Robert Fulghum

Peace is always beautiful.

Walt Whitman

You will show me the path
that leads to life; your presence
fills me with joy and brings me
pleasure for ever.

The Bible

Peace is the fairest form of
happiness.

William Ellery Channing

I don't know what tomorrow holds,
but I know who holds tomorrow.

Author unknown

I have learned the secret of being
content in any and every situation.

The Bible

God takes life's pieces
and gives us unbroken peace.

W.D. Gough